# EXPERIENCE SIMULATION

## A DIRECT ROUTE TO SPIRITUALITY, PURPOSE, AND THE MEANING OF LIFE

GEORGE DUSALA

# TABLE OF CONTENTS

*This book is dedicated to the women, children, and men affected by countless human atrocities all over the world.*

*The pain I feel for them every day is the driving force behind my work.*

*I owe this opportunity to my wife, who has shown me the kind of love I do not want to live without. I also owe it to my mother, who has consistently let me make mistakes, my late father, who always opened my eyes to the truth, and my sister, who has stood with me through thick and thin. Finally, I owe it to all my friends and supporters who have believed in me.*

The contents of this book are aimed at mature, open-minded individuals who are not locked into any particular religion, belief, opinion, or value.

I do not claim to be qualified or competent in any field, nor do I consider myself to have any special abilities, knowledge, or experience. The following are merely open philosophical concepts that have evolved in my mind.

Much of the terminology in this book is taken from various sources of literature, films, music, and other content. I use the terms because many of us are familiar with them. I want the content to be understandable for as broad an audience as possible.

The terms "faith" and "God" are used for the same reason. This is not a book about religion.

As many of us are currently attempting to find meaning in our lives, I wrote this book in an effort to explain the phenomenon we all experience together. This is a short but deep dive into the visible and invisible world around us.

This book aims to help people discover who they are, what they are, and what their purpose is. The goal is to spread genuine happiness, hoping we may one day all thrive together in peace.

# PART ONE
# THE INDIVIDUAL
# PERSPECTIVE

"Earth is a sift through which we are pressed to rid ourselves of impurities."

# CHAPTER 1
# QUESTIONS FROM WITHIN

**Who am I?**

You are the sum of all your previous decisions from all pursued experiences, resulting in a personality that is uniquely you.

---

**What am I?**

You are a sovereign fragment of God composed of pure love. You are also your previous and current intentions.

---

**Where am I?**

You are inside a complex experience simulation we created. The experience involves a human body and various physical abilities and constraints.

---

**Why am I here?**

You are here because you chose to have this experience. You chose this life with this particular set of abilities and constraints.

---

**Why would I choose to come here?**

You and I chose to expand our love intent under the pressure of this reality. This is motivated by the opportunity to grow, which expands our joy and fuels our motivation for future experiences.

---

**Why do I not remember anything before this life?**

We don't remember because a memory veil is in effect. The veil enables us to accept and focus on our current lives.

---

**What am I supposed to do here?**

Expand love by overcoming fear as often as you can. You are here to pursue your highest good through your abilities and use it to bring the highest good to the environment around you. You are here to learn true faith in yourself, which amounts to faith in this reality, which amounts to faith in all realities, which is faith in God.

---

**Why does this sound like the plot of a Hollywood movie?**

It's a message we tell ourselves in various forms and styles. It reminds us to wake up from the spell of our physical senses, cast the animal aside, and find a reason to pursue our highest form.

# CHAPTER 2
# THE EPIC JOURNEY

The universe is a vast network of experience simulations. It hosts worlds and civilizations of every kind and is expanding faster than we can reach the outer limits, making it infinite.

The simulation is a gesture of love; everything inside it falls within a spectrum of love. There are only acts of higher love and lower love.

Our journey begins when we set out into the cosmos to deepen our existence by having an experience. The first experience will likely open doors to other experiences, so the journey rarely ends with the first life. Each life is distinctive in how it impacts us. Each one offers a unique range of experiences, constraints, and opportunities.

As we experience our first realities, we make mistakes that affect us and others. We make them because every reality has some form of constraint. However, being constrained is foreign to new entities, so mistakes inevitably happen. The transition from a perfect painless state to a flawed one builds a natural desire for growth and development.

We choose to have the human experience just like we choose anything while having the human experience. After being shown the exciting possibilities of growth on Earth, we all decide to come. The decision might be easy, or it might not be easy. Some may come for the thrill, some for the beauty, some for the learning, and some to re-learn what they might have forgotten. The scope is endless.

The nature of our existence is additive. Our lives stack onto themselves with each deepening experience helping to fulfill the last while fueling the next.

# CHAPTER 3
## THE EARTH CONTRACT

We agree to walk into the ring of fire, knowing we will emerge transformed. During our time inside the flames, our aim is to love with all our being as often as possible.

The Earth contract is a test of will. It is a polarizing environment designed to squeeze us incrementally. Our progress is measured by the amount of void we are able to bridge and the quality of our intent through the various hardships we encounter.

The distance between what we experience on the inside and what we can project outwards signifies the progress we have already made and the growth we can potentially achieve. When we strive to bridge that distance, powerful new learning experiences are formed.

We are animals physically, but mentally, we are something else. We have a drive to be better than our past selves, and we want to change the world around us in the process. We carry a highly motivated super intelligence that gives us the ability and desire to mold our external environment like no other animal on Earth can.

The combination of survival instinct and a highly advanced logical processing core creates a volatility in each individual, requiring a heightened sense of awareness and deliberate internal maintenance.

# CHAPTER 4
## EVERYTHING IS ALIVE

The simulation does not distinguish between living and non-living matter as we do. Our core inner substance is the same for all matter, regardless of its level of development. We are all Fragments of God.

Everything that can have awareness does because our reality is here specifically to give experience to awareness. Everything living and non-living has awareness because it completes the full spectrum of obtainable experience.

There is a natural hierarchy of experience. We do not take on a life that we are not ready for. Instead of throwing ourselves into extreme scenarios that do not yield much progress, we gradually move up the hierarchy of involvement, with every previous experience readying us for the next experience, maximizing the utility of every life.

Although inanimate objects are little involved in this world, they still experience it firsthand. Objects may not provide sensory data to the experiencer like biological bodies do, but that may be precisely what makes those lifetimes valuable and unique.

The transition to a biological state on Earth represents the readiness to pursue a life with biological constraints. The more sensory data we have, the more potential for constraint, and constraints deepen the experience.

The various animals, plants, and non-living objects in this world are flavors and intensities of experiences available to us, the experiencers.

# CHAPTER 5
## SHAPESHIFTING

Apart from the pains, discomforts, and bodily emotions, the way you feel inside right now is the way you will most likely feel when you die. The transition is subtle. Many of us might not even know we are dead once we are dead. This is because we never actually die. Our existence has no death; it only shifts form.

We do not truly die or truly live (in the biological sense). Life is a compelling dream. After death, the dream is over, but we stay the same. Our additive existence ensures that we will remain fundamentally the same, and our experiences will be fully remembered and integrated.

. . .

Death might come with various negative feelings, emotions, and pains, but they all gradually vanish afterward, much like when we wake up from an actual dream.

Our death can be preordained or simulation-driven. Each type has its use cases, which can be valuable in various ways.

After the Earth Contract expires, we choose where we go. Some of us might want to go directly into another experience, and some might want to return to Source for rest, healing, and transmutation.

# CHAPTER 6
## SOURCE

On Earth, we wear clothes; in Source, we wear our experiences.

Source is the home of the Mind, our awareness. It's the realm where we all exist together. After our life here is over, some go directly into another life, and some do not. For the ones who do not, Source is the place we return to.

Source does not have form except for the form we each attribute to it. Each individual shines their own light and manifests their own environment from memory and fantasy in Source.

. . .

There is no privacy in Source because there is no need for it. We all wear our experiences for everyone else to see. Our past intentions are plainly visible, and communication to others in Source happens transparently. There are no secrets because we all understand the enormous constraints of life, and therefore, we all understand each other's flaws without ever having to inspect them. Love in Source is pure because no constraints are present, and everyone remembers everything from every experience they have ever pursued.

Source serves as a resting ground in which we can help integrate our newest experiences. We integrate by spending time in pure environments or environments that do not impose constraints. These environments are created from memory and fantasy. They serve only to equalize our internal state, providing no additional growth.

The magic wears off after spending enough time in Source, and we inevitably get bored. Our growth depends on casting ourselves out of Source and into reality systems.

# CHAPTER 7
# THE DECISION TREE

The experience simulation is built on finite rules, and everything within it is also finite. Although our awareness is infinite, physical space and time are not. We can make a limited number of decisions in any given lifetime.

The decision tree is the roadmap of our physical existence. It contains all the possibilities for everyone and everything in the universe within a given space and time, including individuals, groups, societies, civilizations, planets, etc.

There are branches in each decision tree, and once you choose a branch, it may be challenging to swap branches because changing your position in the tree means having to reposition others in the tree as well. This brings the speed of manifestation down to a crawl. Consequently, frequent hopping from branch to branch yields little to no results. More time inside a single branch produces forward movement up the branch and up the tree.

This reality's reactions to our inputs are slow but relentless. Once we align ourselves with a branch, we can climb the tree. If it is the right branch, the branch that we are destined for, it will take us all the way to the top, where the light shines the brightest and the fruit tastes the sweetest.

# CHAPTER 8
# FREE WILL AND DESTINY

Fundamentally, we are free will. The choice to have the Earth experience was an act of free will, and the Earth experience itself is an exercise of free will. But we each also have a preordained destiny.

This reality gives us the freedom to choose our steps forward but doesn't give us the option not to make the decision. It allows us to pick a direction, but it does not let us avoid the choice itself, and it will drive us into the ground, past the threshold of the physical if we try to avoid it altogether. This uncompromising wall of force exists because we have already decided to make the choices and ride them out to the very end.

· · ·

Life is a playground of choice. It is a decision tree comprising an enormous but finite number of possible decisions. Our destiny is to make these choices when they present themselves.

Nothing can be done about what we have done and been in the past. The energies we carry are the products of our decisions, and it's our destiny to figure out what they are. Avoiding our destiny is an act of defiance against ourselves and can potentially degrade our existence into the darkest corners of lower love.

# CHAPTER 9
# PREORDAINED

Certain elements must be preordained for this life to give us what we came here for. It is a type of destiny.

Apart from the decisions of others, anything that has the ability to influence us can be predetermined. Like everything else in this life, we choose to face these events for the growth and development they are here to provide.

The framework of preordained events is as complex as the decision tree of which we are each a part. Our destinies evolve in real time and are affected by each decision we make. Each time a direction is picked, our position in the decision tree may be shuffled into a different spot, and the corresponding preordained events start to manifest.

Preordained events will happen no matter what direction we choose, but they will change every time we change directions in our decision tree. Each direction has its subset of predetermined events tasked with reinforcing our goals.

For someone who has not identified their true nature, the idea of being more than the sum of this life can be daunting, and the concept of destiny may seem unworthy of acceptance.

# CHAPTER 10
## PUSH PULL

There is an invisible force pushing and pulling on every human experience. It's a core mechanic that slowly and inevitably churns, helping to align us with the missions we have chosen for this life.

We feel it internally, especially when we are alone. It may feel like a calling to some, while to others, it feels more like pain. It is the Internal Pull. The Internal Pull exists to inspire the self-initiated Internal Push.

The Internal Push is what we are here to do. It requires self-discipline, self-reflection, acceptance, and courage. When we engage the Internal Push long enough, an External Push emerges, working in tandem with our efforts.

The External Push complements our Internal Push by expanding the reach of its positive influence, manifesting abundance.

But if we ignore the Internal Pull, it eventually decays into an External Pull and starts producing events in the physical world around us. These events signal that we are heading in the opposite direction of what we want. The further we go in the unintended direction, the more profound the physical manifestations become, and justifying our course becomes increasingly difficult.

# CHAPTER 11
## DIVINE PROCESSING

The Divine Processing Engine is the system that runs the manifestation of our reality. The system uses our average feelings, intentions, thoughts, and actions as a foundation for our future manifested reality.

This works by examining all our past and current intentions and decisions and, from that, creating a set of assumptions about our future intentions and decisions. Divine Processing works based on careful prediction.

These continuously updated predictions are the foundation of our everyday manifestations. The flow of matter takes a physical amount of time on

Earth, and Divine Processing generally follows the rules of time and space. Manifestation itself has momentum, so changing directions takes time.

But the future can't be fully predicted because people can change their stance instantly. Sometimes, we suddenly decide to do things differently than usual. If we suddenly decide to take on a higher role, things around us begin to shift. If you suddenly decide to do more good in this world, the system starts to scramble in a rapid exchange of priorities, all working to bring you a more appropriate future.

If this event has large enough potential to positively impact others or prevent catastrophe, the system can break its own rule set, distort manifestation, and bridge the gap internally to provide the necessary outcomes.

# CHAPTER 12
# CONFLICTING HISTORY

It's easy for most of us to forget how punishing our natural environment is.

We live in a place that will kill us slowly and inflict excruciating pain if we are not fed and clothed regularly. If we are fed and clothed, life still kills us slowly and most likely exerts pain in the long term. On top of that, we deal with many sorts of internal pressures and pains.

In fact, for some beings, staying fed means having to rip another animal apart in a spectacular display of savage violence. If they do not, this place will kill them slowly and inflict excruciating pain in the process.

. . .

This probably sounds disconnected from our modern lives, but it is precisely what our human bodies have partially evolved from. Survival is part of our genetic makeup, and the survival instinct is with us every moment.

The survival instinct is embedded in every individual and every element of our society. It is present in our homes, schools, hospitals, prisons, and governments, as well as in our friendships, partnerships, and romantic relationships.

When advanced intelligence and animal survival instinct combine, volatility results. Our history may consist of extreme survival and extreme abundance lifetimes. The human experience combines these two opposite poles into one life, and we bear the weight of the difference.

This life clashes our abundance-driven hyper-intelligence with our fear-driven survival instinct. It creates an expansive experience for the individual, a valuable experiment for our collective, and a highly contributing element to our universal growth and development.

## CHAPTER 13
# THE UNDERWORLD

The Earth Contract expires when we complete the work we set out to do, not when our bodies die. Each of us has agreed to a specific state by the end of our journey, and this life is here to give us the means to achieve that state. If we cannot reach the chosen state before physical death, our experience is cast into the Underworld.

The Underworld is an inverted environment that runs parallel to our physical world but contains only the pain and suffering associated with it. It is an extension of this experience, effectively morphing us into our desired state. The Underworld is a last resort for entities seeking to attain the level of growth they initially set out for.

·  ·  ·

Depending on our internal status and outlook, the amount of time spent in the Underworld can range from zero to gargantuan sums.

Every time we commit acts of lower love in our human lives, our ascension collapses. It is not the acts that condemn our experience into the Underworld; it is the slowed development that typically inhabits the actor.

Acts of lower love convolute our journey because they convolute the journey of others. Our experiences are linked, and we are the ones who pay for our actions. We pay with time.

If we refuse our reality, we automatically shift to a state that does not appreciate the gift of life, degrading our whole experience to the lowest tiers of love. We risk not attaining our initial goals if we do this long enough.

The Underworld is not here to punish us but to serve us. It is here to help us achieve our goals, not to cause pain or regret. The Underworld is a gesture of love that catapults our development into our chosen state.

# CHAPTER 14
## GUIDES

Part of the Earth experience is accepting the memory veil. Our memories are wiped clean before each new life so we can focus on that life. Fully knowing our true nature doesn't support our human goals, but not knowing our true nature puts us at risk of losing ourselves and becoming strays of the physical world. It's a double-edged sword.

To counteract this problem, an active communication system, in the form of hints, is created. They are our Guides.

Guides are numbers, words, images, colors, sounds, smells, thoughts, dreams, events, or anything else that can relay a basic message. This message is highly subjective to each individual, and guides will always operate within each individual's current physical and spiritual constraints. Every individual has their own communication channels through which guides can exert influence.

Guides are here to help us through our reality's complex maze. They are a balancing force to our animal, fear-dominant physical nature.

Guides are here to help us align with our true cause. They communicate with us using our physical environment, including our physical bodies. What they try to tell us varies greatly, but their goal is always to breach our wall of beliefs that do not support truth. Our guides aim to destabilize the poorly chosen foundations on which our lives are built so that we may build new and better foundations.

Guides do not have a separate agenda from us, the experiencers. They want what we want. They are extensions of ourselves and our missions and are meant to point us in the direction we want to go.

Once communication between you and a guide has been established, it can grow in complexity over time.

# CHAPTER 15
# FEAR

Fear can take many forms and has many layers. It is the existence of a void we have not filled or an experience we have not fully integrated.

The additive nature of our existence stacks our fears onto themselves over multiple lifetimes. We come here with fears already seated deep within, most of which take the form of various negative emotions, eventually solidifying into mindsets and outlooks.

Fear is also a product of our physical genetics. Our partial history of survival has created habits that are not conducive to love, peace, or acceptance.

The animal inside is still trying to survive even when there is no longer much need for it.

Fear is present in every individual, group, and system. It is the part of us that wants to destroy every risk, including the risk of love, peace, and faith.

One of life's core duties is identifying and expressing our fears for processing and healing. However, this can also be one of the hardest things for an individual to do.

# CHAPTER 16
# PAIN, PLEASURE, AND DEPENDENCY

For some, life has been excruciatingly painful. Giving and receiving love is unimaginably complex, even seemingly impossible. Pleasure can temporarily substitute for pain, providing an oasis from suffering. But before long, that can become the only way to live, consuming the experiencer.

Everything that can provide pleasure has the potential to create dependency. Overcoming this dependency is problematic because it requires delving into the issues that initiated the mindset for it in the first place. It is a spiritual ailment, and the cure requires a spiritual approach.

· · ·

This is not because pleasure is wrong or damaging. Pleasure is a natural counterweight to pain and should be used accordingly. But our decision to substitute pleasure for the giving and receiving of love is another matter altogether.

When faith is at an all-time low, the answer is to serve others, particularly those less fortunate than you. There is always someone less fortunate than you. Service to a higher cause expands our love intent, opening us up to the truth about our world and ourselves.

When we choose to believe in something higher than our own experience, we learn the difference between the pain of discipline and the pain of regret. We also learn that one temporary discomfort can bring long-term good to others, bringing joy to all. Through service to others, we find the value of pain, pleasure, and the healing powers of faith.

# CHAPTER 17
# SELF-TALK

We have a Mind operating in Source. It's almost like a brain but doesn't rely on physical rules. The human brain is a narrow representation of our Mind in Source.

Our Mind is infinite, but our brains are not. This fundamental difference is one of the most challenging constraints in this reality. We are limitless beings learning to act within a set of strict rules.

Our brains are a kind of biological machine intelligence. Reality gives input, the brain processes it logically, and we interpret the result.

Our brains do not possess desire or longing; they do not want.

You, the awareness, are the one who wants. You interpret what the brain outputs.

For many of us, our brains have become the center of our existence. This biological machine has been commandeered to define our day-to-day lives. We have given our will to interpret to something responsible for processing, not interpreting.

We have embraced our brains so intensely that they are where you and I spend most of our days. We talk to ourselves in all sorts of ways, and indeed, at specific points in our lives, we should talk to ourselves. But continuous self-talk is a pleasure-seeking habit; it's a dependency. As such, it is a downward spiral, pulling us further from the truth and deeper into a deluded state.

Living in a false impression, we stop believing in our Mind. We lose faith in ourselves and lose our connection to Source. We step out of the driver's seat and into the passenger's seat, handing over control of this experience to our physical bodies.

. . .

But the body is animal in nature and only knows pleasure or pain. If we let the body take control, we end up losing sight of all that matters to us and slowly embark on a path of destruction and suffering.

# CHAPTER 18
## EGO

Through enough self-talk, we pass into the realm of delusion. It comes in the form of an identity that we construct.

The ego is a term for the system of lies we tell ourselves. If we decide to buy into our lies regularly, we eventually forget that they are lies, and they start to stack onto themselves, forming a complex entity.

The ego is the identity we have successfully sold ourselves through self-talk. It is the ideal we have constructed in our minds. It is the person we see ourselves as or the person we would like to be.

The ego is detached from logic, disconnected from our Mind in Source, and built entirely upon fear.

Our constructed identity has the power to rule us. We can become intoxicated with proving its worth. We start treating our ego like a deity. We begin to defend it. It can become our reason for living.

But in the end, the ego is just a fantasy that we sell to ourselves as truth and the lie we choose to buy.

# CHAPTER 19
## THE FEED

We come to this reality with deep-seated fears from previous lives. We bring them along because resolving them is a big part of the process. We also acquire new fears that, if unresolved, will seat themselves deeper.

Our personal internal experience on Earth is continuously being modified. The Feed is broadcast into our physical minds and bodies. It is the workload we have decided to take on and is one of our central roles in this life.

We process our guilt, fears, and previous actions from this life and prior lives because we need to accept the reality we have created for ourselves and others. Otherwise, it hinders our forward development.

The Feed comes in the form of feelings and thoughts. We are here to interpret, accept, and work through them with positive intentions.

The feed can change every day. Some days, it might be easy, and others, it may be agonizing. There is no pattern to decipher; it is just the workload. If we refuse the workload, it begins to pile up. If we let it pile up too high, our long-term development will slow and deteriorate.

There is no way to get rid of the Feed. There is no quieting or slowing down, only covering and avoiding. We can only try to focus on something else. But before long, the stack collapses, and the workload is forced onto us all at once.

# CHAPTER 20
## THE VOID

Pursuing acts of lower love results in an internal void, which typically takes the form of a deficiency in faith. Creating voids collapses our ascension and increases the time and work it will take to develop ourselves in our chosen direction.

But voids do not simply move us backward and forward. They deepen our experience. Conquering voids adds richness to our existence. It has the power to create complex learning experiences, but it also requires much more effort and is less likely in the long run.

A void is filled when we decide to recognize, accept, and change our intention of lower love.

When an actor of lower love decides to bridge a large enough void, the effects penetrate deep into the surrounding environment. The level of accomplished work internally inspires the masses and raises spirits.

Filling large voids has the potential to move the world around us. Those who carry the deepest and darkest voids have the power to bridge them, giving them the ability to heal the rest of us by the millions through direct non-physical influence.

# CHAPTER 21
## CONNECTED MATTER

Awareness on Earth is a kaleidoscope. At any given moment, our experience involves a combination of our Mind in Source, the human brain, the memory veil, the Feed, Divine Processing, guides, all the physical sensations of the body, and finally, the direct non-physical influence of others.

Direct non-physical influence refers to the internal effects individuals have on each other. It is most felt between people in the same vicinity but not necessarily engaging in verbal communication.

When we share physical space with another, we also share non-physical space. When our non-physical worlds collide, our individual constraint systems temporarily intertwine, and we each get a glimpse into the other's experience. This reality intermingles our differences, allowing us to grow together.

But there is also a war going on.

There is a war on a plane we cannot see. Forces of lower love are battling forces of higher love. The war is happening inside each of us. You and I are soldiers in this war. We each bear our own weight, but we also bear the collective weight of our species. Each soldier has the potential to shift the outcome of the war.

The outcome of the internal war will determine the future of our world. Every individual's mental and spiritual struggle is crucial, particularly those who bridge the largest voids.

# CHAPTER 22
# THE HEART GOES ON

The bonds we form in our lives are real. Like our own experience, relationships are additive, building on themselves over multiple lifetimes. We come to this place knowing specific individuals already, some very deeply. We don't remember each other, but our hearts intertwine from the moment we meet.

Our bond with another grows deeper every time we choose to assume a different mutual role. As strange as it may sound, the deepest bond we can achieve is one that has undergone the most and the biggest variety of simulated relationships.

·  ·  ·

Our relationships may be our first encounters, bonds strengthened by multiple lifetimes of learning, or inextinguishable flames developed by millennia of mutual expansion.

Our love for others stays with us and with them after this life. We bring our bonds back to Source, where we are reunited until the next journey.

# PART TWO
# THE SOCIETAL EXPERIMENT

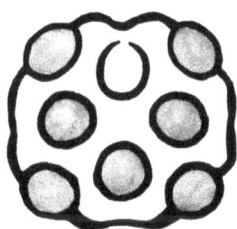

"If today every human on Earth declared war on the worst parts of themselves, tomorrow would be the first day of everlasting peace."

# CHAPTER 1
# AGGRESSIVE EXPANSION

Since the dawn of our time, fear has been the central motivation of humans. However, today's world is changing rapidly, and fear is losing its effectiveness as a motivator.

Our age is experiencing an unprecedented rate of change from a fear-dominant mindset to a faith-dominant mindset. This shift has been happening for a long time, but we seem to be at a very steep point in the transition.

The expansion is affecting the rate at which the consequences of our intentions and decisions manifest individually and collectively. This is putting an elevated strain on everyone, particularly those walking paths they don't want to be walking.

The expansion is impacting the masses. Our society's flaws are becoming increasingly exposed. Events around the world are slowly bringing people to common ground. Our individual objectives seem to be aligning with our true collective purpose.

We appear to be waking up from the dream of our simulation.

# CHAPTER 2
# WAVES OF INFLUENCE

Our species' growth and development occur in waves. It is a process of breathing in and out, alternating between phases of tension and release. This approach ensures that we continue growing and prevents us from regressing.

Every wave of influence develops us in its own distinct way. Faith is lost and found again at every stage. Every societal challenge creates a new void in our collective awareness. When we bridge the void, we grow together as a species and improve our individual and societal functioning.

Because our intentions as societies change as we experience the various waves, new consequences and growth opportunities continuously arise. The variety of waves ensures development across the board, sometimes resulting in irregular growth. But ultimately, growth is the only option, and every wave pushes our species further along in development.

# CHAPTER 3
# RULE OF MAN

Over the millennia, we have attempted various styles of governance. Each attempt has found a way to handle the diverse challenges of managing a human society.

Typically, our governments have been organized in a way that favors and protects the individuals designing the rules of that system. They have used authority, force, and often violence to materialize the ideas of the ruling parties.

Authoritarian systems assume the worst-case scenario for every inhabitant, inside and outside the system. To cope with this fear, they build a structure of force. Over time, this form of governance can erode its society's collective strength and resiliency.

Democracies attempt to allow more freedom, independence, and liberty. They are a closer representation of what we are each fundamentally. Democracy deploys the highest level of faith into society because it willingly takes on the risks of a free society. For this reason, democratic societies are relatively resilient and have a strong collective force.

# CHAPTER 4
# SOFT AND HARD POWER

There are two ways an individual can influence another individual or group: hard or soft.

Hard power relies on sowing fear. It embraces the resource-driven animal mindset. People tend to default to hard power because it is what's coded in our physical genes. It is also the mindset taught to most of us during our earlier phases in life. Hard power tends to be what most leaders employ because it is what they believe in but also because it is what you and I tend to respond to most effectively. Fear of outcome is the motivator here.

Soft power relies on faith. It embraces believing in ourselves, trusting others, and accepting this experience. Soft power uses logic where needed but is not led by logic. Fear of outcome is less important here.

Hard power creates an environment in which people use hard power against each other. This environment becomes a survival habitat, and the animal survival instinct becomes our source of individual power. Those who don't succumb are eventually outmatched and outperformed. Discipline comes in the form of pressure exerted by the fittest.

Soft power produces an environment of friendship, trust, and community. It does not pit individuals against each other but instead encourages deep collaboration. Discipline comes in the form of shared decisions and consequences, acceptance of each other, and mutual expansion.

Hard power requires a structure of control to function. Soft power does not need a control structure because it is internally structured through mutual incentive. Soft power involves faith, while hard power does not.

· · ·

We all use soft and hard power daily, depending on the situation. It is difficult to say whether soft power alone can lead this world, mainly because you and I are so willing to submit ourselves to hard power.

# CHAPTER 5
# CULTIVATION OF BLAME

Life is often not fair, pretty, or kind. Things happen, and sometimes, it can be challenging not to blame. But we are all affected by negativity. We all experience pain and suffering to some degree. Accepting what we cannot change is part of the experience, but most of us cannot accept it, so hate and blame emerge.

Almost everything that has happened in this world until now is a direct result of our collective and individual intentions and decisions. We are all accountable for the reality we are currently experiencing.

. . .

But most of us do not teach or preach accountability. Blame has become the primary way we handle negativity. Mistakes are rarely learned from because they are seldom taken responsibility for. Instead of seeking ways to improve, we seek ways to escape guilt. We have successfully cultivated a culture of avoiding pain at all costs.

At the global level, we blame other countries. At a national level, we blame other political parties. At a local level, we blame other individuals. On a personal level, we blame anything and everything except for ourselves.

Our systems and institutions are run by individuals who suffer from the same things you and I suffer from. Expecting our systems and institutions to be without flaws when they are created, run, and used by flawed individuals would be irrational.

Yet, that is precisely what we do. Instead of fixing our environment, we look to others to fix it. We expect others to do what you and I are unwilling to do. We require our society to be better than us when we don't even want to be better than ourselves.

· · ·

Society leaders will always be an image of the current collective identity composed of individuals like you and me. If that identity revolves around pointing fingers and blaming others, then that is exactly what our leadership will also revolve around.

# CHAPTER 6
# COLLECTIVE CONSEQUENCE

We like to live under the impression that our individual decisions have no impact on society. We believe our systems and institutions should be better than those they represent. But that is not the case.

The quality of our institutions and systems is synonymous with the quality of the average individual. They are the sum of our journeys. The face of society represents the combined internal state of every individual within the society.

We want better government leaders, but we have forgotten to lead our own lives.

· · ·

We want better education, but we keep ourselves intentionally uneducated.

We want a better justice system but are unwilling to do justice in our personal space.

We want people to be honest but we don't mind lying to ourselves and others.

We want others to consider us when we consistently only consider ourselves.

We want less corruption in our systems but have corrupted every corner of our internal world.

The real villain is inside each of us, and our society is paying the price.

# CHAPTER 7
# FRICTION OF SOCIETY

The world is our toolset, but we are also its tool. It uses others to bring us the results we want, and it uses us to bring others the results they want.

Our mission is entangled in the missions of others. Our influence is spread to individuals around us, and their influence is spread onto us.

Each of us possesses a unique set of traits and lacks a unique set of traits, creating a network of mutual opportunity. There is great potential to learn from each other, individually and collectively, and this place makes excellent use of that potential.

·  ·  ·

Our reality uses our strengths and weaknesses to systematically improve our species by continuously creating friction between us through our encounters. The tension that emerges ultimately serves to expand everyone involved.

For the system to work effectively, every other system must be connected. Our anatomy, geography, demography, ethnicity, and other traits that make us collectively unique are all deliberately patterned and work in unison with our experiences.

# CHAPTER 8
# THE GRAND PUZZLE

Our species is scattered around this planet in patterns, not randomly. The local geography, climate, fauna, flora, and non-living objects are intrinsically linked to our regional identity.

All elements sharing local space are connected, creating groupings. We have created borders around some of these groupings to separate our differences.

Our various nations, cultures, and ethnicities have strengths and weaknesses. Society experiences friction, much like friction between individuals. This friction occurs on a collective scale, allowing progress to be made individually and collectively.

. . .

No nation, race, gender, ethnicity, or tribe is without fault. We rely on each other to prosper.

The human race is split up into a collection of various puzzle pieces. It is no coincidence that we fill in each other's blanks. The challenge is finding a reason to accept our mutual differences, learn from the strengths of others, and be willing to look into our own weaknesses openly. If we can build ourselves into the whole of what we truly are as a species here on this globe, there are no bounds to what can be accomplished.

Isolation is not the way forward. It does not lead to the place we would like it to lead. It only steers us toward further self-degradation.

We all want to live, we all want to love, we all want to learn, we all want safety, we all want freedom, and we all need food and shelter. Our shared human needs couldn't be clearer. Finding common ground is the key.

# PART THREE
# SOWING THE SEEDS OF TOMORROW

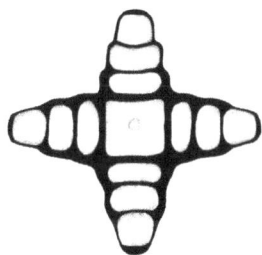

"All you can do in this life is to try and make a paradise for yourself and a paradise for others."

# CHAPTER 1
## TURN YOUR BRAIN OFF

Self-talk has become an epidemic in the human race. The age of information has accelerated the exposure of a truth present in every individual: the infinite nature of our awareness. But our brains are not infinite. And that difference poses a serious problem for us all.

Don't turn your brain off completely; turn off certain behaviors so others can flourish. Delegate the task of logic processing to the logical processing unit, your brain, and take back the power of interpretation. It belongs to you.

Separate yourself from the simulation of your brain and body. Become an observer.

. . .

Gain a good understanding of your internal activity. Observe your mind and gain a solid grasp of what goes on inside regularly. Get very well acquainted with your thought patterns, but only as an observer. Do not judge your thoughts or assign value to them. Let them flow freely.

Allow time for the information to sink in. Repeat the process until you have a solid image of your daily mind chatter.

Accept the good and the bad from your findings. This can be particularly challenging, so give it the time and effort it needs.

Create a system of discipline for your human mind. Become the ruler of your brain. Wage war against your thought machine if you have to. Use whatever tools you have to regain control of your intelligence, and the Mind will start flowing inward from Source.

Build the type of environment you want to live in every day, inside your mind. Make it a place you

want to spend time in, and your life will transform
overnight.


Free yourself from the prison of your human mind
and start living a life worth living to the fullest.

# CHAPTER 2
# SET YOUR INNER CHILD FREE

The inner child speaks from a place of peace and tranquility. It only wants the joy to flow outwards indiscriminately. There are no needs; there is no agenda. The child only wants to play.

Do not confuse this with your animal impulses. Although the two may sometimes feel similar, they are not. This reality does a great job of entangling them.

Each of us has an inner child. It is not a separate entity; it is us without the external effects of this world. It is us before we indoctrinate ourselves into our physical reality and convince ourselves of whatever we have convinced ourselves of.

. . .

The child can see the clearing through the thick undergrowth. It recognizes the impostors in this game. The child knows what we have forgotten and how to remember it again.

But the inner child is the part we want to grow up from. We do this to be more practical. And many of the efforts are, in fact, very useful and practical.

The problem isn't that we want to be useful. The problem is that we discard the entirety of our inner child, the good and the bad. We refuse the inner child because we choose to measure its worth in pure practicality. We quantify its value with logical reasoning and automatically cast doubt on the precious abilities of our inner child.

But we are the child. It is us without our baggage. The inner child is our purest element. Set your child free.

# CHAPTER 3
## ACCEPT YOUR FATE

You made your fate when you decided to come here with all the energy your personality brings.

You are not here to be anything you want to be. You are already what you are, which most likely extends far before and beyond this life. You come with talents, gifts, abilities, and many more positive traits. But you also come with more cynical qualities.

Embrace all of your negative energies. Do not feed your bad habits, but rather take a long, hard look at who you are and who you have been. See the far-reaching consequences your behaviors have created.

. . .

Try to understand that this life is only part of who you are. You may have certain traits that this life cannot explain alone. Accept the ones from this lifetime, and accept the ones not from it. Do not compare them; they are all you.

Do not lie to yourself. Learn to recognize the difference between legitimate reasons and excuses. Call yourself out like you may want to call someone else out. Seek truth in every moment. Try to see the essence in every encounter.

Stop running from yourself. Let your guilts drown you. You must face them head-on. Accept yourself, accept your fate, and you will find that accepting others comes naturally thereafter.

# CHAPTER 4
## DEFINE YOUR VALUES

Our uniqueness is what sets us apart on this journey. We should embrace our personalities, the good parts and the not-so-good parts. We must find the positive side of every negative aspect. It's there, waiting to be seen.

Do not let this world tell you what you are and what you are not. Don't give others the power to declare what is appealing, what has purpose, and what the meaning is, because all of that belongs to you. You are the one defining and living your life; no one else can live or define it for you.

You live the consequences of your decisions, not the decisions of others. You do not have to take on the opinions and values of others to bring them happiness. You do not have to put on a facade of behavior to give others joy. You do not have to destroy your humanity to provide humanity to others.


Let the individuals in this world live their lives from their perspectives, and let yourself live your life from your perspective. Become the main character in your story, embrace your uniqueness, and define the values that make your life yours.

# CHAPTER 5
## GET IN YOUR LANE

We all contain something that makes us valuable to our environment.

Other people's stories may seem more interesting, but anybody can make a story appear or sound interesting. You are the only one who gets to experience your life from your perspective, and the story you make about yourself is the one you get to live and take away.

Do not give others the power to set your standards. Form a set of values and then judge yourself based on those values.

· · ·

Discover what burns the brightest inside you. Seek the things that move you and make you want to change the world. Illuminate the shadows of your fears, bring them out into the spotlight, and embrace them.

Find your lane and get in it. Step outside your comfort zone, stride into the unknown, and take a leap of faith.

Be patient; it might take time. It may have to happen in phases. You will probably make mistakes along the way. Try to embrace the process; it's working for you. Whatever happens, stay on course, even if in small increments. Your lane will remain open for as long as it can.

# CHAPTER 6
# EMBRACE CHANGE

Change amounts to growth and is one of the core purposes of life on Earth. Through change, we experience the learning and expansion we have decided to pursue. But for many of us, change is also the enemy.

Many of us try to remove ourselves from the process entirely. However, avoiding change is much more costly than the change process itself, partially because there is no long-term reward for avoidance and partially because of the terminal nature of the pain.

The friction between individuals and societies has deeply confused us. The discomforts we feel from seeing and feeling the differences between ourselves and others drive us into a state of mutual hostility. This hostility creates barriers between what we want and what we can achieve.

Embrace the pain of being less than your rivals, mentors, and friends. See the gap between what you are, what they are, and what you want to be. Let the pain guide you in deciding what you want to change most about yourself and your experience.

# CHAPTER 7
## LET YOUR GUIDES FIND YOU

You have spent your entire life in this reality and know what happens to you daily. No one can tell you what you see because only you can see it from your perspective.

Are you experiencing patterns? Do you keep seeing or hearing something specific? Are there certain thoughts going through your mind regularly? Do you keep smelling the same scent in different places? Does a particular kind of animal continuously visit you?

It's essential to consider this retrospectively but not actively use it to find future phenomena.

Doing so would primarily result in fantasizing about guides and not actually letting them see us.

This strangeness exists because guides cannot be observed, so we can't look for them. They must find you, but you must be open to their existence for them to see you. And that, you may find, is quite a challenge.

Unfortunately, there is enormous potential to drift into the realm of imagination while seeking Guides. Our brains are intelligent and deceptive. Allow yourself to become curious. Try not to judge. Recognize the guide from your fantasy. Discern what you experience very carefully.

This can be a long process. Do not expect things to move quickly if you have spent your whole life not believing in guides. Let your ideas tumble around until only a select few remain. Things will become more apparent, and the most important concepts will eventually step on stage if you let them.

Regular communication with guides can become part of your daily life with enough time and faith.

# CHAPTER 8
## BE IN THE NOW

Life is always happening in the present moment. However, our past and future have pivotal roles to play. The role of the past is self-reflection, and the role of the future is projection. Both roles are essential to our growth and expansion.

Self-reflection is the act of honestly and genuinely examining our past decisions and actions. Every action has consequences, and we must be willing to truthfully inspect our past and the consequences it has brought into the present. Without self-reflection, the drive for growth eventually decays into a desire for power and pleasure.

· · ·

Projection is imagination or spontaneous fantasy. It significantly affects our future manifestations, so we must be careful about what we project. Like self-reflection, projection is a powerful tool we can learn to utilize effectively. However, if we do not guide our projections voluntarily, they still happen involuntarily. The outcomes of involuntary projections may not align with our true intentions, so staying aware and guiding our projections is essential.

Both self-reflection and projection can be twisted and abused. What may begin as a spiritual journey can quickly transform into fantasy and lies. We must stay vigilant because our brains continuously attempt to deceive us.

# CHAPTER 9
# LOVE YOUR EXPERIENCE

The existence of the universe is an act of love. Experience simulations are built on love and fueled by faith. Gratitude for what we already have is the foundation on which everything else is built.

Do not blame your experience for your struggles. Do not let your negative feelings conspire against your perspective on this life. If you need to find something to blame, stand in front of a mirror and keep standing there until you find it.

Start facing your experience from a place of gratitude. Our internal gratitude opens the door to the invisible network of faith. Something is always being given to us, so pay close attention and do not take it lightly.

Populate your environment with people and things you want to fight for and die for. Build out your experience with ideas and concepts you want to believe in. Accepting others is key, but accepting ourselves and our unique personalities is just as important because it lets us personalize our experience. Personalization makes our lives more manageable, resulting in abundance.

Accept help. Giving and accepting help are acts of courage. You are not here alone and are not meant to live alone. Welcome the fact that we need each other.

Be as kind to yourself as you try to be to others. Discover the importance of respecting yourself.

Create a vibe inside that you want to live every day. Define your paradise, build your internal world around it, and protect it with everything you have.

# CHAPTER 10
# THE FUTURE IS ABUNDANT

The human experience has steadily grown in abundance over the ages. Compare our modern lives with an average life in the Middle Ages; the difference is jarring. Although our development is not linear, it is the only thing we know. Forward is the only direction we can go.

The question isn't whether we will grow or not. The question is whether we can evolve as a species without destroying ourselves.

We are walking the line. Our society is at the cliff edge of our future existence. The situation on our planet is highly volatile because it is also highly volatile inside each of us.

. . .

We must each take responsibility for our journey and face our reality directly. If we can achieve this individually, we can achieve it as a society.

Imagine a society where people don't have to labor every day just to have the opportunity to live. Imagine if our schools allowed children to roam freely and engage naturally. Imagine if our prisons helped individuals reintegrate and become better human beings. What if our energy sources were limitless, our food security everlasting, and our communities safe and supportive?

War would be reduced to a game. Politics would become a comedy entertainment show. Borders would cease to exist, and there would be only one unified government: a government of the people.

If you and I learn to leverage ourselves, our societies may one day retire fear and enlist faith as the new normal. If we can overcome our fears, this reality can slowly be replaced by one in which we all want to thrive in peace. If our societies learn to leverage effort and faith simultaneously, we as a species will one day overcome our inner traumas and will make it to our abundant future.

What we do from this point on will determine the future of the human race.

Our future is waiting.

.

# AFTERWORD

Being human is an opportunity. Our lives are not mandatory; they are voluntary. The experience simulation is a grand gesture of love.

Every moment is a gift, whether we can see it in the moment or not. Facing our reality directly with arms wide open is the way we will make our lives purposeful, the way we will discover true faith in our existence, and the way we will create everlasting happiness for ourselves and our surroundings.

May your journey lead you to the places you are meant to be, the people you are meant to see, and the individual you are meant to become.

www.ingramcontent.com/pod-product-compliance
Lightning Source LLC
Chambersburg PA
CBHW060207070426
42447CB00035B/2792

*9 7 9 8 9 9 2 6 5 8 0 0 2 *